RUG

Story and Pictures by Mary Rayner

There was once a dog called Rug.
He was big and shaggy.

He was an Old English sheepdog.
He lived with a girl called Nicky.

One day they went for a walk.

Rug liked walks.
He liked to roll in the mud.

He liked to run around,

he liked to run after things.

First he got very muddy,

then he saw some sheep.

The sheep saw Rug.

They ran away.

Rug ran after them.

"Baa, baa, baa," went the sheep.
"Woof, woof, woof," went Rug.
"Rug, Rug, Rug," went Nicky.
"Bad dog, come here."
But Rug kept on running.
He thought it was fun.

The sheep did not think it was fun.
They were afraid.
They ran to the other side of the field.
Rug ran around and chased them back.

Nicky ran too.
"Rug, Rug, Rug," called Nicky.
"Bad dog, come here."
The sheep ran back again.
"Baa, baa, baa," went the sheep.
"Woof, woof, woof," went Rug.

Nicky caught Rug. She was angry.
"Bad, bad dog," said Nicky.
She put him on a leash and took him home.
"I am going to bathe you," said Nicky.
"You don't like baths.
It will serve you right."

Nicky bathed Rug.

He did not think it was fun.

"All better," said Nicky.
"Now you are a clean dog."

The next day Rug and Nicky went for a walk again.
They met the farmer.

"Morning," said the farmer.
"I saw a dog like yours yesterday,
an Old English sheepdog.
He was running after my sheep.
But he was not clean and white and fluffy like yours,
this one was brown and shaggy.
Do you know anybody with a dog like that?"

"Oh," said Nicky.
The farmer said, "If I catch him at it
again, I will take him to the dog pound."
"I will keep my eyes open," said Nicky.

"Thanks," said the farmer.

"Whew!" said Nicky.
"Rug, you must never chase sheep again."

"Woof," said Rug.
And he never did.

This edition first published in the United States in 1989 by Gallery Books, an imprint of W.H. Smith Publishers, Inc.,
112 Madison Avenue, New York, New York 10016. Produced for Gallery Books by Joshua Morris Publishing, Inc. in
association with William Collins Sons & Co. Ltd. Text and illustrations copyright © 1989 by Mary Rayner. All rights reserved.
ISBN 0-8317-4422-7 Printed in Hong Kong.